40 Things To Know When You Are 40

www.40thingstoknowwhenyour40.com

Copyright © 2024 H N Comyn

All rights reserved. No part of this book may be reproduced, distributed, or transmitted in any form or by any means, including photocopying, recording, or other electronic or mechanical methods, without the prior written permission of the author, except in the case of brief quotations embodied in critical reviews and certain other noncommercial uses permitted by copyright law. For permission requests, please contact the author through info@40thingstoknowwhenyour40.com

Published by Hazel Comyn
Ireland
ISBN: 978-1-0685771-1-6

Disclaimer: This book is intended to provide helpful and informative material on the subjects addressed. It is not intended as a substitute for professional advice. The author and publisher specifically disclaim any liability that may be incurred from the use or application of the contents of this book.

Cover and Interior Design: Hazel Comyn

Dedicated to all the people stressing out about turning 40. It's really not as bad as you think!

Contents

1. The "Life Begins" Philosophy
2. Did You Just Discover The Secret About Confidence
3. Life's Playlist Gets a Remix
4. Sleepless in Your 40s
5. Old Dogs, New Tricks: Still in the Game
6. The Hours You've Clocked
7. Body Reboot: New Features Unlocked
8. Wanderlust Chronicles
9. The Sleep Struggle Is Real
10. Food For Thought: Lifetime Edition

11.
Blink and You'll Miss It
12.
A Lifetime of Chatter
13.
Heartbeats Counted and Pumped
14.
Pop Culture Time Machine
15.
"Over-the-Hill" Shenanigans
16.
Global 40
17.
Midlife Crisis or Transition
18.
Your Ears and Nose: Still Growing Strong
19.
Welcome to Puberty 2.0
20.
The Incredible Shrinking You

21.
Sudden Culinary Plot Twists
22.
Midlife Mirage Moments
23.
Body Sounds: Now in Surround Sound
24.
Your Brain's Age-Bending Tricks
25.
Senses on Shuffle
26.
The Phrases You Didn't Realize You'd Adopted
27.
Pulled Muscle: The Sneezing Edition
28.
Comfort Over Fashion: No Regrets Edition
29.
The 40-Year Achievement Unlocked
30.
The Curious Case of Exploding Head Syndrome

31.
Phantom Phone Vibrations: It's a Thing
32.
Wine Face: Aging's Secret Side Effect
33.
Midlife Migraine Mysteries Unraveled
34.
Hot and Cold: Temperature on Turbo
35.
Bingo Wings in Unexpected Places
36.
The 40-Year-Itch: It's No Myth
37.
Wisdom Teeth 2.0
38.
Metabolism: Now in Slow-Mo
39.
A Dollar a Day Keeps Regret Away!
40.
The Karaoke Curse: 40's Unseen Encore

1. The "Life Begins" Philosophy

Don't fear turning 40—embrace it, because this is when life truly comes alive. It's not an ending; it's the beginning of a thrilling new chapter, where you finally get to write your own story. You've spent years gathering experiences and wisdom, and now you're equipped to navigate life with a boldness and clarity like never before.

This is your moment to chase passions, set audacious goals, and make choices that resonate with your deepest desires. Let go of what anyone else expects—this is your time to live authentically and unapologetically. Turning 40 isn't just another year; it's the launchpad to something extraordinary. Your best years have only just begun!

2.
Did You Just Discover The Secret About Confidence

Turning 40 is like stepping into your power—finally, you've reached that exhilarating point where you can say, "I've got this," and truly mean it. You've navigated life's twists and turns, learned from every stumble, and come to realize what truly matters to you.

The magic of your 40s isn't just in knowing more, but in knowing yourself. You've shed the weight of worrying about what others think, and embraced the freedom to live life on your own terms. It's about breaking free from the cocoon of self-doubt and emerging as the most authentic, unapologetic, and fiercely amazing version of yourself.

This surge of confidence isn't about having life all figured out (because newsflash: no one does!). It's about trusting that you can and will rise to meet whatever comes your way. It's laughing in the face of challenges, letting go of the small stuff, and filling your life with what lights you up. Whether it's rocking a daring new look, boldly saying "no" without a second thought, or diving into a new passion just because it excites you—your 40s are your time to shine.

So step boldly into this decade, radiating joy and self-assurance. You've earned this freedom to embrace life fully, to own your story, and to live each day with a smile that says, "I'm just getting started.

3.
Life's Playlist Gets a Remix

Turning 40 is like hitting shuffle on your priorities, and guess what? It's the best remix yet! The things that once seemed so urgent—climbing the corporate ladder, chasing the latest gadgets—start to fade into the background, making way for what really makes your heart sing. You realize that time is the most precious currency, and you'd rather invest it in moments that bring genuine joy: savoring quality time with your favorite people, diving into a hobby you've always dreamed of, or simply getting lost in a great book—guilt-free.

It's not about giving up on your ambitions, but about leveling up your mindset. You start to say "yes" only to what fuels your soul and "no" to what drains it. You become a master of tuning out the noise and tuning into what matters most.

Self-care is no longer an afterthought; it's a non-negotiable. And work-life balance? It's no longer a cliché, but a way of life that you fiercely protect.

You've uncovered the secret that life's too short to be tangled up in the trivial. Instead, you zero in on the essentials— happiness, health, and creating memories that last a lifetime. The beat goes on, and you're dancing to the rhythm of your own song, making every moment count.

4. Sleepless in Your 40s

Ah, sleep in your 40s—it's a bit of a love-hate relationship, isn't it? You might find yourself waking up at 3 a.m. for no apparent reason, or suddenly feeling the urge to nap at 2 p.m. (Seriously, when did naps become a thing again?) Hormones, stress, or even that second cup of coffee can start to play tricks on your sleep patterns. It's like your body has decided that sleeping through the night is overrated, and you're left wondering why you can't just get that sweet, uninterrupted sleep you used to take for granted.

But here's the fun part: it's the perfect excuse to embrace some new bedtime rituals! Think comfy pajamas, soothing teas, or even that fancy pillow you've been eyeing. You might also find that winding down without screens or establishing a calming bedtime routine actually works wonders. Sure, sleep may not come as effortlessly as it once did, but that doesn't mean you can't enjoy a good snooze. And if all else fails, there's always the joy of a perfectly-timed weekend nap—because at this stage, you've definitely earned it!

5.
Old Dogs, New Tricks: Still in the Game

Learning new skills in your 40s is like unlocking your inner kid again—only this time, you've got the patience to stick with it! Whether it's mastering a new language, strumming a guitar, or finally figuring out what all those fancy cooking terms mean, now is the perfect moment.

Your 40s come with a unique mix of wisdom and a "why not?" mindset. You know what you love, and you're not afraid to dive in headfirst just for the sheer fun of it (even if it means a few laugh-out-loud beginner moments along the way).

The best part? You're not here to impress anyone but yourself. That's the magic ingredient. Who cares if you stumble a bit at first or if you're the oldest one in the class? You're doing it for the thrill of learning, the joy of a new challenge, and the satisfaction of shaking up your routine.

Trying new things keeps your mind sharp and adds a little extra spice to everyday life. So go ahead—sign up for that painting workshop, join a salsa group, or even give coding a whirl. Because who says your 40s can't be the most adventurous, fearless decade yet?

6.
The Hours You've Clocked

By the time you celebrate your 40th birthday, you will have lived through approximately 14,610 days. That's counting the leap years that came around every four years, adding a few extra days to the mix. It's a journey spanning four decades, where each day brought new experiences, memories, and growth.

If you break it down even further, those 14,610 days translate into about 350,640 hours. That's over 350,000 hours of laughter, challenges, milestones, and everyday moments that make up the fabric of your life. Those hours have been spent working towards goals, sharing conversations, exploring new places, and finding time for relaxation and reflection.

When you dive into the minutes, you've experienced around 21,038,400 minutes—over 21 million moments that could have been filled with anything from the mundane to the extraordinary. Each minute is a tiny piece of your timeline, some spent in anticipation, others in joy or sorrow, but all together creating the rich tapestry of your life.

And then there are the seconds—approximately 1.26 billion seconds to be exact. That's 1.26 billion heartbeats, breaths, and blink-and-you'll-miss-it flashes of time. Each second is a pulse of life, ticking away, carrying you forward, and building up to this very moment. It's incredible to think that such a massive number is composed of countless small instances, each one shaping your journey to 40.

7.
Body Reboot: New Features Unlocked

By the time you reach 40 years old, your heart will have worked tirelessly to keep you going, beating approximately 1.5 to 2 billion times, depending on your average heart rate. If your heart has been beating at around 70-80 beats per minute on average, it's pulsed day in and day out, keeping your blood circulating and your body thriving.

That's about 100,000 heartbeats a day, each one a quiet reminder of the life force within you, adding up to billions of beats over four decades. Through every moment of excitement, stress, exercise, and rest, your heart has been a constant, unceasing rhythm in the background of your life.

When it comes to your hair, it's grown more than you might expect. Over the years, your hair has gradually extended about 23 feet (7 meters) in length if you consider a typical growth rate of half an inch (1.27 cm) per month. That's a steady 6 inches (15 cm) per year, accumulating to a length that could stretch nearly the height of a two-story building.

From haircuts and trims to letting it grow out during different phases of your life, those millions of hair strands have kept regenerating, contributing to a remarkable total length over time.

And your skin? It's been constantly renewing itself, with approximately 800 full skin renewals by age 40. Given that the skin cell cycle averages about 28-30 days, your body has gone through hundreds of mini skin transformations, shedding old cells and generating new ones. That means your skin has essentially reinvented itself every month, continuously working to protect you from the elements, heal cuts and scrapes, and adapt to the changing conditions of your environment.

Your heart, hair, and skin have been quietly but steadily at work throughout your life, performing their everyday miracles without you even noticing. Together, they've carried you through the ups and downs, reminding you of just how remarkable the human body truly is.

8. Wanderlust Chronicles

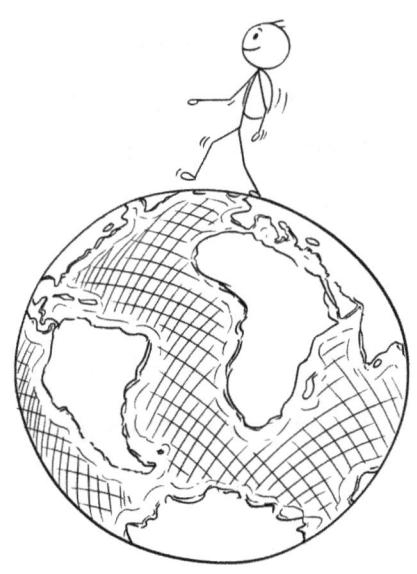

By the time you turn 40, you've embarked on a cosmic journey of around 23.3 billion miles through space. That's because the Earth, orbiting the Sun at an average speed of 67,000 miles per hour, covers a staggering 584 million miles every year.

Without even realizing it, you've been traveling through the vast expanse of our solar system, carried along for the ride as our planet makes its annual journey around the Sun.

Over the course of four decades, that adds up to a truly mind-boggling distance—enough to circle our solar system many times over!

On a more down-to-earth scale, if you've been averaging about 7,500 steps per day, then you've taken over 109.5 million steps in your lifetime.

That's millions of strides taken across different terrains—whether strolling through city streets, hiking nature trails, or simply moving through your daily routine.

It's an impressive number that shows just how much ground you've covered, quite literally, one step at a time.

All those steps add up to approximately 55,000 miles (or 88,500 kilometers), which is more than enough to walk around the Earth's equator twice.

Imagine tracing the entire circumference of our planet not just once, but two times over, using only your feet!

Those miles represent countless journeys—both big and small—that have carried you through life's adventures, from your first steps as a child to every exploration and everyday movement that followed.

9.
The Sleep Struggle is Real

If you've been averaging a solid 8 hours of sleep each night, then by the time you reach 40, you've clocked in about 13.3 years—yes, years—of your life nestled in bed, catching those precious Zs. That's more than a decade spent resting, recharging, and letting your body and mind recover.

Think about it: while the world was awake and buzzing, you were deep in the land of slumber, laying the foundation for better health, clearer thinking, and more energy.

But there's more happening in those 13.3 years than just sleep—you've also been dreaming. And not just a few dreams here and there; you've likely experienced around 52,000 dreams!

The average person dreams about 3 to 5 times each night, meaning you've had an entire library of vivid, strange, beautiful, and sometimes downright bizarre adventures playing out in your mind. From flying over cities to reliving cherished memories, these nightly voyages have filled your sleep with moments that are anything but ordinary.

Those 52,000 dreams are more than just random images—they're reflections of your experiences, hopes, fears, and everything in between. They've accompanied you through different stages of life, weaving in elements from your past and even offering glimpses into the future. Each one is a tiny story, a window into your subconscious that's been open nearly every single night of your life.

So, while you've spent over a decade asleep, you've also been on countless mental journeys, proving that even in rest, life never truly stops unfolding.

10.
Food for Thought: Lifetime Edition

Assuming you've stuck to the classic three meals a day routine, you've devoured around 43,800 meals by the time you hit 40. That's a whole lot of breakfasts, lunches, and dinners! But here's where it gets really interesting: if you spend an average of 1 hour per meal, that adds up to roughly 4.4 years of your life dedicated solely to the art of eating.

Think about it—4.4 years spent savoring flavors, indulging in your favorite dishes, and sharing countless meals with friends and family. Whether it's cozy Sunday brunches, hurried weekday lunches, celebratory feasts, or comfort food on rainy nights, those hours aren't just about feeding your body—they're moments woven into the story of your life.

And that's not just time at the table. It's memories made over holiday dinners, laughter shared during backyard barbecues, and even the quick bites on the go that have fueled your day-to-day adventures.

You haven't just been eating; you've been living, one meal at a time.

11.
Blink and You'll Miss It

By the time you reach 40 years old, your eyes will have blinked approximately 620 million times, based on an average blink rate of about 15 times per minute. That's a lot of blinking!

Considering there are 1,440 minutes in a day, this means you're blinking roughly 21,600 times daily, which adds up quickly over the decades.

Each blink, though brief—lasting only about one-tenth of a second—serves an important purpose.

Those millions of blinks have kept your eyes lubricated, clearing away tiny particles and providing a shield against dust, wind, and light.

They've helped maintain your vision by refreshing the surface of your eyes every few seconds, ensuring that you can see clearly throughout the day.

Think about all the moments those blinks have spanned: from every sunrise and sunset you've witnessed, to all the pages you've read in books, screens you've glanced at, and faces you've seen.

Each blink is a tiny, unnoticed act of self-care that's happened continuously, even while you weren't consciously aware of it.

So, while you've spent just a fraction of your life in the act of blinking, those 620 million blinks have played a quiet but vital role in keeping your world in focus.

12.
A Lifetime of Chatter

By the time you are 40, you've probably spoken around 860 million words—that's enough to fill thousands of books or narrate an epic, lifelong conversation.

Think of all the stories you've told, the jokes you've cracked, and the heartfelt moments you've shared. Those 860 million words have been your soundtrack, carrying you through every debate, heart-to-heart, and spontaneous burst of laughter. You've used your voice to express love, convey ideas, and sometimes even win a few arguments along the way.

And as for your voice itself, it's a bit of a shape-shifter. Around the age of 40, it may start to undergo some subtle changes. For some, it becomes a little deeper and more resonant, thanks to the thickening of the vocal cords.

For women, this often means a slightly lower pitch, lending a tone that's richer and more textured. For men, the voice may develop some subtle fluctuations, creating a sound that's uniquely seasoned by the years.

These changes aren't just signs of aging—they're like a vocal badge of honor, marking the experiences that have shaped who you are. Your voice carries the story of your life, evolving just as you have, growing stronger, deeper, and more authentic with every word.

So embrace the power of your 860 million words—speak boldly, laugh loudly, and let your voice be a reminder that you've got a lifetime of stories worth sharing.

13. Heartbeats Counted and Pumped

By the time you hit the big 4-0, your heart—a true MVP working 24/7—will have pumped approximately 1.4 million gallons (or 5.3 million liters) of blood. That's no small feat! To put it in perspective, that's enough to fill over two Olympic-sized swimming pools with the life-giving liquid that's been coursing through your veins since day one.

Your heart doesn't take breaks, clock out, or call it a day—it just keeps on pumping, beating 100,000 times a day, tirelessly moving blood through a network of arteries, veins, and capillaries that stretches around 60,000 miles. Every heartbeat, every gallon pumped, has kept you thriving—powering your muscles, fueling your brain, and carrying oxygen and nutrients to every corner of your body.

Think of it this way: you've been carrying around your own personal fountain of youth, a perpetual motion machine that's been with you through every rush of adrenaline, every moment of calm, and every time your heart raced with excitement. With 1.4 million gallons pumped and counting, your heart's story is one of resilience, strength, and unwavering dedication.

So next time you feel that pulse, give yourself a little credit. Your heart has been putting in the work to keep you living boldly, loving deeply, and embracing every beat of this incredible journey. Let that be your inspiration— because if your heart can pump enough blood to fill swimming pools, there's no limit to the life you can live!

14.
Pop Culture
Time Machine

In the span of 40 years, you've been riding the ultimate tech rollercoaster! You went from the days of cassette tapes and VHS—when rewinding with a pencil was a legit skill—to the age of streaming and smart devices that let you control your whole world with a swipe or a voice command.

You've lived through five generations of gaming consoles, starting from 8-bit pixels and blocky graphics to virtual worlds that look almost real. If there was ever a Hall of Fame for tech evolution, you'd be in it!

And let's not forget about the music scene. From the days when disco fever ruled the dance floors to the rebellious grunge of the '90s, and now the digital age where you can summon any song ever made in a split second.

You've watched genres transform, merge, and evolve, becoming the soundtrack to every chapter of your life —from mixtapes made for crushes to today's playlists curated by algorithms.

Turning 40 means you've also witnessed the rise of an entire cultural phenomenon—social media!

You were there for the birth of MySpace back in 2003, where picking your top friends was a serious life decision, and now you're scrolling through today's endless feeds of TikTok dances and Instagram stories.

You've lived through the entire evolution, from when social media was just a novelty to it becoming a way of life.

So here's to you—the ultimate tech and culture survivor, who's seen it all and isn't done yet. You're proof that age is just a number, but experience?

That's pure gold. Keep evolving, keep adapting, and keep living life in full HD.

15.
"Over-the-Hill" Shenanigans

Turning 40? Now that's a global adventure worth celebrating! Let's take a delightful tour around the world to see how this milestone is honored.

In Germany, hitting the big 4-0 isn't just a number; it's a whole vibe! This birthday is often celebrated as a major leap into midlife, and you can expect a healthy dose of "over-the-hill" humor.

Friends love to pull off surprise parties filled with playful pranks, cheeky jokes about aging, and a guaranteed good time.

So, prepare yourself for laughter, laughter, and more laughter—who knew turning 40 could be so much fun?

Now, hop on over to the U.S., where 40th birthdays bring out the "over-the-hill" theme in all its glory! Imagine a bash decorated with black balloons and tombstone cakes—yes, it's all in good fun! Expect to hear plenty of jokes about getting older as everyone embraces the humor of aging. It's a celebration that reminds you that while you might be climbing the hill, the view just keeps getting better!

Meanwhile, in the U.K., the approach to 40 is a bit more refined. Here, folks often celebrate with dinner parties or special gatherings among close family and friends.

This is a time for reflection, with heartfelt speeches and toasts that honor life's achievements. So grab a glass and toast to the fabulous journey that has brought you to this point— cheers to the next chapter!

Traveling south to Mexico, milestone birthdays turn into fiestas filled with family, music, and mouthwatering traditional food.

For the big 40, get ready for a lively celebration complete with mariachi music, dancing, and all the joy that comes with appreciating life. It's a reminder that turning 40 is not just about getting older; it's about embracing every moment with gusto!

So, no matter where you are in the world, turning 40 is a spectacular reason to celebrate. With laughter, joy, and a sprinkle of nostalgia, this milestone marks not just a new age but a fresh chapter in your incredible story. Get ready to party!

16.
Global 40

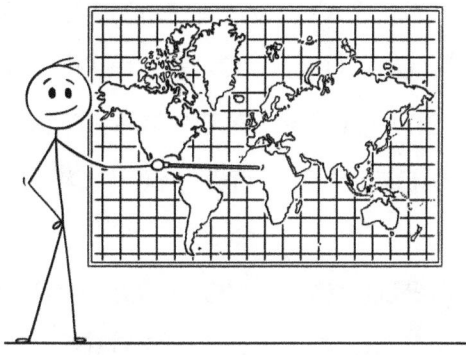

In Japanese culture, hitting the big 4-0 means entering the realm of "Yakudoshi," where this age is seen as a bit unlucky for men.

But fear not! Special rituals are in place to banish the bad vibes, and family and friends throw fabulous celebrations to shower you with protection and blessings for the year ahead.

It's like getting a lucky charm with a side of confetti!

Over in Korea, turning 40 marks the beginning of "Hwan-gap," a milestone that celebrates completing one full cycle of the traditional 60-year zodiac calendar.

While it might not be as grand as the big 6-0, it's still a fabulous opportunity to reflect on all your amazing achievements and plot out your next adventure.

Think of it as a gentle nudge to take stock and aim higher!

In India, this age is cheekily dubbed the "Naughty Forty," and boy, do they know how to celebrate! Picture elaborate parties bursting with music and dancing, all infused with a carefree spirit.

It's a time to embrace life with fresh enthusiasm and maybe even a little mischief—because why not?

In China, reaching 40 is all about wishing for long life and good health. Celebrations are filled with delicious noodles—because who doesn't want to slurp up some longevity?

Red decorations are everywhere, symbolizing good luck and prosperity, making your special day feel like a festive parade of positivity.

And then there's Russia, where some might choose to keep things low-key when turning 40.

Superstitions suggest this age can be a bit unlucky, so rather than a big bash, you might find folks opting for cozy celebrations with close family. It's the perfect excuse to enjoy the company of loved ones without all the fanfare.

So whether you're warding off bad luck, embracing the naughty side of life, or simply savoring noodles, turning 40 is a chance to celebrate in style—each culture adding its own unique flair to this fabulous milestone!

17. Midlife Crisis or Transition

If you're suddenly gazing longingly at a sleek sports car or daydreaming about a bold career switch, congratulations— you might just be riding the wave of a classic midlife crisis!

But fear not; this isn't just about impulse buys and moments of existential panic. Oh no, my friend! A midlife crisis is simply a fabulous opportunity for a life makeover.

Think of it as a fun little audit of your existence—like checking your GPS to see if you're still heading toward your dream destination.

This is your moment to check in with yourself and see if you're still cruising down the road of passion and happiness.

Are your dreams still aligned with your day-to-day reality? If not, it's time to shake things up!

And let's be clear: you don't have to make radical changes (though if that convertible calls your name, who's going to stop you?).

Sometimes, it's the little tweaks that can make a world of difference.

Consider picking up a new hobby that ignites your spark, planning a trip to that far-off place you've always wanted to explore, or finally saying "yes" to the things that light you up and "no" to the stuff that drains your energy.

The beauty of a midlife crisis is that it's a playful invitation to rediscover who you are and what you truly want—without the weight of seriousness holding you back.

So, embrace the chaos and have a blast! Life's too short not to enjoy the ride, so put on your favorite tunes, hit the gas, and let this midlife adventure lead you to new and exciting places!

18.
Your Ears and Nose: Still Growing Strong

It's a wild and wacky truth: while the rest of your body may decide it's time to hit the brakes on growth, your ears and nose are the overachievers in the aging game! Thanks to gravity and the slow breakdown of collagen and cartilage, those once dainty features start to stretch and expand. By the time you hit the fabulous age of 40, you might catch yourself doing a double take in the mirror, wondering if your ears are auditioning for a role in a cartoon!

But don't fret! This quirky phenomenon is all part of the journey we call aging. Instead of viewing your larger-than-life features as something to cringe at, think of them as badges of honor! Your ears are not just catching sounds; they're catching wisdom. Your nose? It's become a seasoned navigator, guiding you through the aromatic adventures of life.

Just picture it: every wrinkle and every new curve tells a story of laughter, joy, and the incredible moments you've experienced. And let's be honest—those oversized ears? They could easily become your secret superpower, amplifying all the wonderful things around you, from the laughter of loved ones to the latest gossip!

So, as you embrace this new chapter and these subtle changes, wear your beautiful, evolving features with pride. You're not just growing older; you're growing richer in experience, charm, and character. Your ears and nose may be on a growth spree, but it's your spirit that truly takes center stage. So celebrate every unique aspect of you—after all, life is too short to not embrace your fabulous self, nose and all!

19. Welcome to Puberty 2.0

Ah, the fabulous 40s! A time often heralded as the beginning of a new chapter—filled with wisdom, adventure, and, surprisingly, a sprinkle of puberty all over again!

Yes, you read that right! Hormonal changes around this age can sometimes bring about symptoms that might make you feel like you're reliving your teenage years—complete with mood swings, unexpected acne, and even changes in body odor.

It's like your body decided to throw a nostalgia party, and you're the guest of honor!

As you cruise into midlife, your body's estrogen and testosterone levels can start doing the cha-cha, leading to those delightful mood swings that can transform you from a serene Zen master to a fiery whirlwind in seconds flat.

One moment you're laughing at a funny meme, and the next, you're tearing up over a commercial for cat food—what gives?!

But hey, let's not forget about the rebellious skin! Just when you thought you'd said goodbye to those pesky breakouts, your face decides it wants to join the "Acne Revival" tour. It's a reminder that your skin is as dynamic as your life journey—constantly evolving, just like you!

And let's chat about body odor. Your sweat glands might just be cranking up the volume on their production, leading to some unexpected olfactory surprises.

Think of it as your body's way of saying, "Hey, we're in this together! Let's keep things interesting!"

But don't let these hormonal hijinks get you down! This transitional phase is an incredible opportunity to reconnect with yourself.

Embrace the rollercoaster ride of emotions as a sign of your vibrant spirit! Instead of fighting against these changes, lean into them. They're simply signals that you're entering a new phase of life, full of possibilities and growth.

So, if you find yourself with a pimple on your chin or suddenly craving pickles at midnight, laugh it off! Celebrate the quirks and embrace the journey.

This is your time to shine, navigate the waves of change, and come out the other side even more fabulous than before. Remember, the best is yet to come, and every twist and turn only adds to your unique and vibrant story!

20.
The Incredible Shrinking You

Hold onto your hats (or maybe your heels)—because as you glide into your 40s, you might start noticing something a little unexpected: you may be getting shorter! Yes, it's true! This phenomenon isn't due to any magical shrinking ray but rather the natural compression of your spinal discs. Think of it as nature's way of reminding you that while you're aging like fine wine, your spine is just going through a little "collapsing" phase.

Now, let's unpack this: your spinal discs are like the cushions in your favorite chair, designed to keep you comfy and supported. But as the years roll by—especially as early as age 30—these cushions start to lose their plumpness. By the time you reach your 40s, that loss of height can become more noticeable, and you might find yourself approximately half an inch shorter for every decade you cruise past.

But fear not! This isn't a sign that you're shrinking into oblivion; it's simply a gentle nudge from your body that it's time to prioritize your health and well-being. Instead of viewing this change as a setback, see it as an opportunity to focus on the incredible experiences and wisdom you've amassed over the years. After all, the height of your spirit and your achievements are what truly define you!

Think of it this way: with each passing year, you're not just losing inches; you're gaining perspective! It's a chance to embrace new adventures, explore new horizons, and stand tall (even if it's not quite as tall as before).

And here's where the fun really begins! Why not invest in some fabulous shoes that give you that extra lift, or try yoga to strengthen your core and improve your posture? Not only will this help you feel more grounded, but you'll also enhance your overall confidence. Plus, who doesn't love a little extra flair in their step?

So, as you embark on this exciting decade, remember that while you might be losing a few inches, you're gaining a lifetime of experiences, stories, and a vibrant spirit that can't be measured in centimeters. Own every inch of who you are, and let your personality shine even brighter! Life's a wild ride—so let's keep standing tall, no matter what!

21. Sudden Culinary Plot Twists

Here's a plot twist for your 40s: food intolerances or allergies might pop up out of nowhere, even if you've enjoyed certain foods all your life.

As we age, the body's enzymes may decrease, and the immune system might react differently, suddenly making foods like lactose, gluten, or even some fruits feel like unwelcome guests at the table.

It's as if your digestive system decided to shake things up and surprise you!

But don't let this dampen your spirits—think of it as a chance to get creative in the kitchen.

It's the perfect excuse to explore new ingredients, dive into alternative diets, and discover recipes you never knew you'd love.

With so many delicious and healthy options available, this shift can open up a whole new culinary adventure.

So, if you find yourself navigating around new dietary restrictions, embrace it as an evolution in your food journey.

It's not about giving up—it's about leveling up, fueling your body in fresh ways, and savoring every bite of this exciting new chapter.

Midlife isn't about limits—it's about exploring flavors that make you feel amazing!

22. Midlife Mirage Moments

Here's a midlife surprise that's a little offbeat—literally! "Midlife Hallucination Syndrome" is a quirky phenomenon where some people in their 40s catch fleeting glimpses of things that aren't really there or hear a sound that seems to come out of thin air. But before you start thinking your imagination's gone wild, rest assured—this strange little quirk is usually harmless and comes with some very down-to-earth explanations.

These phantom sights or sounds tend to pop up during times of stress or sleep deprivation. It's as if your brain decided it needed a little extra entertainment or a quick reality check while you're burning the candle at both ends. Think of it as your mind's way of saying, "Hey, let's slow down for a sec!" or "Maybe it's time for a nap?" It's a friendly reminder from your own head that a little rest and self-care go a long way.

And sure, catching a glimpse of something from the corner of your eye or hearing a phantom doorbell can feel a bit strange, but it's also a signal that you're living life full-throttle and your brain is working overtime to keep up. Embrace it with a sense of humor—after all, if life's a movie, then these tiny blips are just bonus scenes in your blockbuster.

So, if you find yourself momentarily startled by a phantom sound or sight, take it as a cue to pause, breathe, and tune back into your own well-being. It's your body's quirky, imaginative way of reminding you to prioritize rest, manage stress, and keep your mind as healthy as your hustle.

After all, why not add a little mystery and magic to your midlife? Who says the everyday can't have a few surprises sprinkled in? Embrace it as part of the wild, wonderful ride that's called living life fully in your 40s!

23.
Body Sounds: Now in Surround Sound

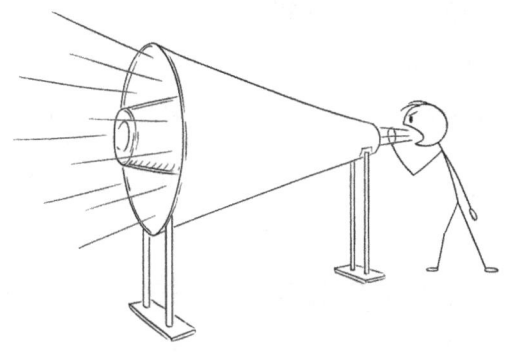

As you stride into your 40s, don't be surprised if your body starts making pops, cracks, and even the occasional grind. These quirky noises are just part of the journey and are nothing to panic over. It's not that your body is falling apart; it's just developing a little more "character" in the process!

These sounds typically come from reduced joint lubrication or a bit of cartilage wear and tear—the kind of stuff that happens when you've been living life fully and putting your joints through decades of dance moves, workouts, and adventures. Your joints are basically saying, "Hey, we've been around the block a few times!" Every click and pop is a little reminder of all the amazing things you've done and can still do!

And just because there's a little more snap, crackle, and pop in your step doesn't mean you're slowing down. In fact, it's the perfect excuse to get proactive about taking care of your body. Make it an opportunity to embrace stretching, try yoga, or dive into some gentle mobility exercises. After all, you're not just aging—you're leveling up, finding new ways to keep your body feeling great and moving with grace.

So, instead of seeing these sounds as signs of age, celebrate them as badges of experience. Let every little creak remind you that you're still here, still moving, and still making your mark. Because at the end of the day, it's not about avoiding the noise; it's about embracing the music your body makes and dancing boldly into midlife with a joyful heart and a playful spirit.

24. Your Brain's Age-Bending Tricks

Around 40, your brain might just decide to hit the refresh button, bringing about some curious changes that feel a bit like a second adolescence. Scientists have discovered that this period can involve a rewiring of the brain's emotional control centers, leading to some unexpected shifts.

Suddenly, you might find yourself feeling bold and spontaneous, with a renewed urge to explore life's possibilities and say "yes" to experiences you've never tried before.

It's as if your brain is shaking off the dust and hitting the gas on adventure mode—you could find yourself taking up new hobbies, diving into projects with a passion you haven't felt in years, or even making impulsive choices that you thought were reserved for your younger days.

Don't be surprised if you start acting "younger" than your age, craving novelty and a bit of fun that breaks up the routine. This isn't a midlife crisis; it's a midlife awakening, where you rediscover the thrill of living outside your comfort zone.

This stage can actually be an exciting opportunity to reconnect with the more carefree version of yourself.

Embrace it as a time to challenge what it means to be "middle-aged" and shake things up. It's not about chasing youth; it's about rediscovering the joy and curiosity that make life vibrant. Your brain is giving you a gentle nudge, reminding you that it's never too late to reignite your passions and reinvent yourself.

So, if you find yourself suddenly inspired to learn a new language, join a dance class, or even switch careers, don't hold back. Let this spark be your guide to making the next chapter of life your most exciting one yet.

Because turning 40 isn't about winding down; it's about revving up and proving that the best is still to come.

25.
Senses on Shuffle

By the time you hit 40, your taste buds might decide to take an early retirement, leading to a reduced ability to savor some flavors—especially sweet and salty. But don't worry, it's just your palate inviting you to explore bolder tastes! You might find yourself craving spicier or more flavorful foods, diving into new cuisines, or adding an extra dash of hot sauce to liven things up. Think of it as your taste buds' way of saying, "Hey, let's make this interesting!"

At the same time, your sense of smell could become a bit of a drama queen. Thanks to hormonal changes, certain scents might start hitting you differently—some odors you once enjoyed could now seem too intense or downright unpleasant. It's as if your nose is going through its own little rebellious phase, suddenly developing strong opinions on what it does and doesn't like.

But here's the upside: this shift can wake up your senses, encouraging you to experiment with new flavors, fragrances, and experiences. It's an opportunity to rediscover the world with a fresh perspective, embracing foods, aromas, and spices you may have overlooked before.

So, go ahead and spice up your life, and don't be afraid to try something new—because your midlife taste revolution is just getting started!

26. The Phrases You Didn't Realize You'd Adopted

You Start Using Phrases Like "I Remember When That Cost Half as Much" in Every Conversation.

"Back in my day..." Perfect for reminiscing about how things used to be, whether it's prices, music, or technology.

"I can't stay up that late anymore." A common response when someone suggests a late-night plan.

"My back is killing me." Because those aches and pains seem to show up out of nowhere.

"I can't believe it's already [insert month]." Time just seems to fly by a little too quickly now.

"Kids these days..." Typically used when observing younger generations doing something you find puzzling or amusing.

"I need to check my calendar." Suddenly, scheduling even social events becomes a must.

"It's too loud in here." Often said when you find yourself in a noisy restaurant or crowded event.

27. Pulled Muscle: The Sneezing Edition

Ah, sneezing in your 40s—who knew it could be a full-body workout? One moment, you're just minding your own business, and the next, you're sneezing so hard that you pull a muscle in your back or neck. It's like your body decided to add a little drama to an otherwise ordinary event.

You used to sneeze without a second thought, but now, every sneeze feels like a mini-exercise in dodging a potential muscle strain. Who knew that "sneeze prep" would become a thing? But hey, it's not all bad—at least you're getting an unexpected reminder to stretch more often! It's a sign that maybe your body is calling out for a little extra TLC.
So, embrace it with humor.

For women in their 40s, sneezing can sometimes come with a little surprise—a tiny bladder leak that wasn't there before. It's a common experience, thanks to weakened pelvic muscles from childbirth, hormonal changes, or simply getting older.

But here's the thing: it's nothing to be embarrassed about! It's just another reminder of how amazing the female body is, handling life's changes with humor and grace. If a sneeze or a good laugh comes with a little extra, consider it an invitation to embrace self-care, strengthen those muscles with some pelvic floor exercises, and keep living life to the fullest—no matter what!

28. Comfort Over Fashion: No Regrets Edition

In your 40s, the comfort-over-style shift happens like magic—and honestly, it's a total game-changer. Those sky-high heels and skinny jeans that once seemed essential start gathering dust in the back of your closet, making way for cushy sneakers and stretchy pants.

Suddenly, you find yourself asking, "Does this outfit have pockets?" or "How soft is this fabric?" more than worrying if it's runway-ready. And you know what? It feels fantastic!

Comfort becomes the new cool, and you start embracing clothes that let you breathe, move, and actually enjoy your day without secretly counting down to the moment you can change into pajamas.

It's not that you stop caring about how you look; it's more about realizing that life's too short to suffer through a day in scratchy, restrictive fabrics.

You can still rock a stylish look—just with a bit more practicality and a lot less pain. Think of it as leveling up in fashion wisdom; you're not sacrificing style, you're just upgrading it with a generous dose of common sense. Because really, what's more stylish than feeling good in what you're wearing?

29.
The 40-Year Achievement Unlocked

At 40, Harrison Ford landed his iconic role as Han Solo in Star Wars: The Empire Strikes Back, which catapulted him to international fame and solidified his status as a Hollywood legend.

At 40, supermodel Christie Brinkley appeared on the cover of the Sports Illustrated Swimsuit Issue for the third time, proving that age is no barrier to success in the modeling world.

At 40, Henry Ford established the Ford Motor Company, which went on to revolutionize the automobile industry with the introduction of assembly line production and affordable cars.

At 40, Leonardo da Vinci finished one of his most famous works, The Last Supper, which has since become one of the most celebrated and studied pieces of art in history.

40, Samuel L. Jackson's career took a major turn when he played Jules Winnfield in Pulp Fiction, a role that earned him critical acclaim and launched him into stardom.

30.
The Curious Case of Exploding Head Syndrome

It may sound like something out of a cartoon, but "Exploding Head Syndrome" is far less explosive than it sounds. It's a harmless (yet startling) phenomenon where, just as you're drifting off to sleep, you might hear a sudden loud noise, like a bang or a crash, that seems to come from nowhere.

Don't worry—there's no actual explosion, just your brain's quirky way of dealing with the transition to sleep. While it becomes more common in your 40s, it's a gentle reminder that even as you age, your mind still knows how to keep things interesting. Think of it as your brain's dramatic way of saying, "Goodnight, world!" before you drift off to dreamland.

31.
Phantom Phone Vibrations: It's a Thing

Phantom Phone Vibrations – they're like your body's version of a ghost story. In your 40s, it's surprisingly common to feel that familiar buzz in your pocket, only to realize there's no call, no text— no phone even there!

This quirky experience, known as "phantom phone syndrome," tends to pop up more as we get older, thanks to a mix of stress, our ever-growing dependence on technology, and that constant itch to stay connected.

It's your mind playing tricks, but it also serves as a little reminder: take a break, unplug, and let life vibrate for real. After all, there's a whole world out there that doesn't need a notification.

32. Wine Face: Aging's Secret Side Effect

In your 40s, you might notice that even a single glass of wine can leave you with a rosy glow—but not in the way you hoped. Welcome to "Wine Face," where your skin decides to get a little too festive. It's not just the buzz; as you age, your body metabolizes alcohol differently, leading to flushed cheeks, a bit of puffiness, or blotchy patches that weren't part of the plan.

It's your skin's way of saying, "Hey, I've been around long enough to react to the little things." But don't let it hold you back—just think of it as your body's reminder to enjoy that sip mindfully, stay hydrated, and embrace the glow, whether it's from the wine or your inner spark!

33. Midlife Migraine Mysteries Unraveled

Welcome to the "Midlife Migraine Mystery," where your head decides to keep you guessing. If you've been a lifelong migraine sufferer, you might just get lucky in your 40s as those pounding headaches finally decide to pack up and leave.

On the flip side, if you've never dealt with migraines before, midlife might throw them your way as a new, unwelcome surprise. It's all thanks to the hormonal rollercoaster that comes with this phase of life, which can flip your pain sensitivity like a switch.

But don't let it get you down—consider it an opportunity to tune into your body's signals, make some lifestyle tweaks, and find new ways to nurture your well-being. After all, even your headaches are just another reminder that you're evolving—and still ready to conquer whatever life throws at you!

34.
Hot and Cold: Temperature on Turbo

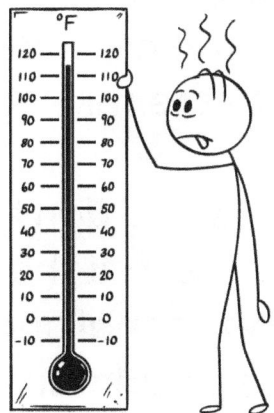

Brace yourself for the body temperature rollercoaster, because in your 40s, things can heat up—or cool down—without warning!

And it's not just about those infamous hot flashes linked to perimenopause; men and women alike can suddenly find themselves battling mysterious temperature swings.

One moment, you're reaching for a sweater, and the next, you're fanning yourself like it's the middle of summer.

These sudden shifts don't always have a clear cause, but they can be triggered by hormonal changes, stress, or even your metabolism kicking into overdrive (or taking a little nap).

Embrace these mini heat waves and chilly spells as a reminder that your body is still adapting and evolving.

You're alive, you're dynamic, and you're keeping things interesting—who said 40 couldn't be spontaneous?

So, whether you're layering up or peeling off, just ride the waves with a smile because change means growth, and you're definitely growing stronger and wiser every day!

35.
Bingo Wings in Unexpected Places

As you glide into your fabulous 40s, you might notice a new addition to your body's portfolio of quirks—say hello to the charmingly dubbed "knee wings!" Yes, that's right! Just when you thought sagging skin was reserved for your arms, gravity decides to throw a little surprise party around your knees.

This phenomenon, often called "knee wrinkles," is all about your skin's natural aging process and its delightful dance with gravity.

Those once-firm knees might start showing some love handles of their own, transforming into wings of wisdom. But fear not! This isn't just a sign of aging; it's a testament to all the wonderful experiences you've had while living life to the fullest!

Instead of hiding those knees under long pants, celebrate them! Rock those shorts or that cute summer dress with pride. After all, every wrinkle tells a story, and your knee wings are a badge of honor, marking your journey through life's ups and downs.

Embrace this quirky twist of aging as a reminder that you're not just getting older; you're getting more incredible with every passing year! So strut your stuff and show off those knee wings—because you're still fabulous, and age is just a number!

36.
The 40-Year-Itch: It's No Myth

Welcome to the intriguing world of the "40-Year-Itch!" Picture this: you're cruising through your fabulous 40s, living your best life, when suddenly—bam!—you find yourself scratching like you've got a secret itch that just won't quit.

You glance around, and nope, no rash, no bug bites, just you and your skin throwing an unexpected party!

What's going on? Well, it turns out your skin is having its own midlife crisis! As you age, changes in skin nerve sensitivity can cause random bouts of itching that feel like a prank your body is playing.

Combine that with the natural dry skin that often comes with this decade, and you've got the perfect recipe for a mysterious scratch-fest.

But don't let this little nuisance get you down! Think of it as your body's quirky way of reminding you to pay attention to your skin. It's time to invest in some luxurious moisturizers or indulge in a calming bath infused with your favorite essential oils. Treat yourself to that self-care routine you've been meaning to try!

So the next time you find yourself in an intense scratch-a-thon, take a moment to laugh it off. After all, you're not just getting older; you're adding a new layer of character to your journey!

Embrace the "40-Year-Itch" as a part of the adventure—because aging may bring a few surprises, but it also brings wisdom, grace, and the chance to celebrate every fabulous moment!

37.
Wisdom Teeth
2.0

Surprise! As you journey through your fabulous 40s, you might find yourself facing a dental twist that could rival any plot twist in a movie: a second set of wisdom teeth! Yes, you read that right! While it's a rare phenomenon, some lucky (or not-so-lucky) individuals actually start sprouting what are known as supernumerary teeth—essentially, a bonus set of wisdom teeth that can make your mouth feel like a crowded party!

Now, this isn't just your average dental drama; this bizarre occurrence can be linked to genetics. So, if your parents had a mouthful of extra chompers, you might just be following in their toothy footsteps. Imagine the surprise during your next dental check-up when the hygienist casually mentions that you've got some unexpected guests in your gum line!

But fear not! While this may sound alarming, it's not the end of the world. Think of it as a quirky badge of honor, proof that your body continues to surprise you in ways you never imagined. If you find yourself on this unexpected dental adventure, consider it a chance to reconnect with your inner teenager, battling for space in your mouth just like those teenage wisdom teeth did.

And remember, every tooth—whether it's one of the original three or a new challenger—tells a story about your journey. So, embrace this eccentricity! Channel your passion for self-expression and maybe even start a toothy blog titled "Wisdom Teeth: The Sequel!" After all, who doesn't love a little extra wisdom on this wild ride called life?

38.
Metabolism: Now in Slow-Mo

Welcome to your 40s, where your metabolism decides it's time to take a well-deserved break! That burger you used to devour without a second thought?

Now it feels like it's sticking around for a while—literally. Yes, your metabolism has slowed down, and suddenly those extra snacks seem to be making themselves right at home.

But don't worry, it's not all bad! It's just your body's gentle reminder that maybe it's time to tweak your habits a bit.

Think of it as an invitation to rediscover balanced eating and find workouts you actually enjoy (hello, yoga and dance classes!).

The good news is, you don't have to give up everything you love—just enjoy it in moderation.

The key is to embrace a few healthy changes, like adding more whole foods and regular movement to your routine, without letting the scale dictate your happiness.

And hey, there's a certain freedom that comes with knowing you're not chasing a "perfect" body anymore; you're simply aiming for a healthy, happy one.

So, laugh it off, keep moving, and remember, life's too short not to enjoy the occasional slice of cake—even if it means an extra walk later.

39.
A Dollar a Day Keeps Regret Away!

If you had tucked away just $1 every single day since the day you were born, by your 40th birthday, you'd be sitting on a cool $14,610 (yes, accounting for those leap years too)!

That's more than just spare change—it's the foundation of a small fortune built from sheer consistency. Imagine the possibilities: a dream vacation, an investment in your passion project, or a generous gift to yourself that says, "Hey, I've earned this!"

It's proof that even the tiniest habits can lead to monumental results. Every day counts, and so does every dollar. Saving one dollar might seem small in the moment, but 40 years later, it adds up to a powerful lesson in perseverance.

This little treasure is a reminder that big dreams start with small steps, and the journey of financial freedom begins with one simple decision to save.
So, what will you do with your $14,610? The choice is yours—just don't underestimate the power of a single dollar and the magic it creates over time!

Imagine extending the $1-a-day habit to your kids and grandkids. By setting aside just a dollar daily for them, you're not only gifting them a future fund of $14,610 by their 40th birthday but also instilling a legacy of smart saving and the power of small, consistent actions. It's more than just money; it's teaching the value of patience, wise financial choices, and building a lasting legacy.

A simple dollar a day can set the stage for big dreams and endless possibilities across generations.

40. The Karaoke Curse: 40's Unseen Encore

Every culture spins its own tales about hitting life's milestones—30 is the new 20, 50 is the prime of life, and 60 ushers in newfound wisdom.

But what they don't tell you is that turning 40 comes with a secret rite of passage that's as baffling as it is real: The Karaoke Curse.

No one warns you about it, and no one believes it exists—until it strikes. It's that sudden, inexplicable urge to belt out your favorite tunes with a passion you haven't felt since your teenage years.

Whether you're a shower singer or someone who once shied away from the mic, 40 brings a magnetic pull toward karaoke stages everywhere.

It's not just a midlife crisis; it's a full-on musical awakening, where the lyrics seem deeper, the melodies sweeter, and your air guitar skills suddenly legendary.

Embrace the Karaoke Curse—your 40s just gave you an encore you didn't know you needed!

www.ingramcontent.com/pod-product-compliance
Lightning Source LLC
Chambersburg PA
CBHW060836050426
42453CB00008B/722